Desire to Inspire

A 100 Day Motivational Book for Women

My desire is that this book will help you to discover, or re-discover your strength, your worth and encourages you to be your best self!

O'Nesseia R. Edmondson

ISBN 979-8-67454-759-4 Softcover

Printed in the United States of America

This book is dedicated to the strong women in my life:

To my mom, Viola, who has always been there for me through thick and thin.

To my beautiful baby girl, O'Riyah, whom I pray will grow up to be a strong, mighty woman of God.

Also, to my sisters Vanessa, Kerry and Keleish my editor, and my spectacular Sisters-in-law who have totally become sisters.

Finally, to my nieces and friends.

<u>Acknowledgement</u>

I would like to extend my deepest gratitude to:

- ➤ God my Saviour for being so gracious unto me and for giving me the opportunity to write this book with the hope that it will uplift women everywhere.

- ➤ To my husband, Oral Edmondson, you have been a constant source of strength, support and encouragement.

- ➤ Hope McCardy, a lady I call my spiritual mom, who prays without ceasing and always have an encouraging word for me.

- ➤ To some sisters that have been a tower of strength to me throughout my journey; Noralee Longley, Marsha Watson-Howlette, Nicola Garwood- Mussington, Karlene Barton, Nadine Edwards-Thomas, Leisa Mohan-Dakari, Simone Reid, Suzette Xeminess, Karene Rogers, Lerone Richards, Annalecia Allison, and Shakia Peet. Thanks to you ladies for being a friend and for always encouraging me to be my best self.

- ➤ To the ladies in both of my small groups at Home Church, in Alberta, Canada.

➢ To those EA beauties I met this year at Gateway Christian School; I'm so happy that I got the opportunity to meet all of you ladies. Thanks to Lynnette and Natalie for posing with me for the cover image and for consenting to the public use of their photo.

➢ Finally, to all the women who will read this book, and find strength and encouragement to be your best self.

Love without Limit!
You ladies are strong and you are rocking this!

Love O'Nesseia

Introduction

This 100-day motivational book, along with my 366-day devotional, *"As His Spirit Leads"*, was born out of years of praying and asking God to give my life purpose! I've prayed and cried out to him in the midst of feeling empty and useless. This was His answer to my cry. This book is covered from front to back with words of encouragement, affirmation and hopefully healing. I believe that God will use this book to nurture the hearts and spirits of my sisters who are broken and bring them back to life. It is also a good reminder to those who are standing strong to continue to strive and remember to pull another sister along with you.

This book has been written with related Bible scriptures as well as a few lines at the end of each entry so that you can meditate and draft a note to yourself (maybe a note of action).
My hope is that this book will become a personal diary for you, engrossed on every page; encouragement, scripture and your own personal entry. I am hoping that this book will become one of your favourites that sit close to your bedside and acts as a constant reminder about what you have written and the promises you've made to yourself. I pray that as you read, God will release

His mighty power over your life and that you will find the strength you need to become the best version of, 'you'!

I ask one thing as you begin this book; that you take it one day at a time. Don't rush ahead no matter how tempting it becomes. I believe if you can do this then after 100 days you will see a significant change in the way you approach life and the things concerning you!

Content

x

Desire to Inspire

A 100 Day Motivational for Women

Day 1

<u>You are Beautiful</u>

Today, look in the mirror and see the beauty that God has created in you. You are chosen. You are royal. You are God's beloved daughter. Marvel at what He has created you to be and do not apologize for being you! Take the time today to breathe, take a stroll, sit in the park, and watch the animals come and go. Do nothing! Today is yours, seize the moment and love upon yourself! I'm taking this opportunity to start by pouring in your spirit, your schema, your intellect.

You are beautiful, intelligent and you are a leader!

Trust His promises to you today. He said He will never leave you nor forsake you, so don't sweat it! You have the greatest of the great in your corner and He's on your side, so launch out. Today is the beginning of the rest of your beautiful life!

> Psalm 46:5 (NIV) God is within her; she will not fall;
> God will help her at break of day.

Note to self:

____

____

____

____

____

____

Day 2

<u>Believe in Yourself</u>

The world sometimes thinks that because we are women, we are somehow inferior. Oh, how I beg to differ. We are strong and resilient. We can juggle home and work like it's a matter of 'frying eggs.' Today, stand tall and proud, and let the world know that you believe in yourself and that you are not intimidated by men, work or a challenge!

God has given you all the tools to go forth and impact your world, whether that is in the work place or right there in your own home.

Today you have my vote for woman of the year. You have more within you than you yourself can ever imagine. Have faith. You got this!

Philippians 4:13 (NIV) I can do all this through him who gives me strength.

Note to Self:

____

____

____

____

____

____

Day 3

<u>You are a Natural Leader</u>

It is simply amazing how a woman can balance home, kids and a solid full-time career. God has made you strong and you are rocking it. You have the ability to conquer any obstacle and rise to the top even if it is with one shoe in your hand, shirt out and make-up running.

At the end of the day, what matters most is that you didn't give up and you made it to the end; end of the day; end of the course; end of the project. Whatever your current battle is, hold on to God's unchanging hand. You are not alone in this season. I am there with you, and remember, you are strong!

Psalm 28:7 (NIV) The LORD is my strength and my shield; my heart trusts in him, and he helps me. My heart leaps for joy, and with my song I praise him.

Note to self:

____

____

____

____

____

Day 4

<u>Smart & Creative</u>

Isn't it amazing how we come up with the most unique ways to get multiple tasks done at the same time? We are moms, teachers, doctors, career women, wives and the list goes on. We can't afford to do one task at a time so we become super women. We get creative and figure out ways to balance it all. And since failure is not an option, we end each day tired and weary, but the success of the day makes it all worthwhile, and before we go off to bed we are already planning for the next day. The ridiculously, insane amount of work that we have to get done within a 24-hour span is crazy, but it's always a blast, isn't it? Another opportunity to show the world just how 'super' God made you! My sister, hats off to you. You are a true force of nature. God loves you and He is empowering you so you can continue to empower those you love.

Psalm 91:4 He will cover you with his feathers, and Under His wings you will find refuge.

Note to self:

____

____

____

____

____

____

Day 5

<u>*Matters of the Heart*</u>

We are sometimes classified as weak because 'heart,' matters to us, but it is because of our heart that we are so versatile. We know just how to love our kids and spouses while appropriately teaching, correcting and even accepting that some things just aren't worth fighting about. We are anything but weak! We are smart and innovative. We are loving and respectful. We think about Christ's heart and that is who we emulate. His heart is big and open, always loving, always forgiving and that's how we women are as well!

Whatever it is today that you need to make a, 'matter of the heart,' go ahead and do it. Trust your heart!

Philippians 4:6 (NIV) Do not be anxious about anything,
but in every situation, by prayer and petition,
with thanksgiving, present your requests to God.

Note to self:

____

____

____

____

____

Day 6

Celebrate Your Accomplishments

Don't be afraid to celebrate the things you've worked so hard to accomplish. Some people would want to silence you and to put a damper on your spirit, but you know who you are and to whom you belong. He gave you the strength to do what you do so celebrate, shout, and let the world know, you are proud of who you are and what you've done. It's not becoming prideful and pompous. No, it's giving God the glory and celebrating the blessings that He has upon your life.

Don't apologize for what God is doing in and through you. If He didn't want you to have this, then He wouldn't have given it to you. So, enjoy it!

1 Corinthians 15:10 (NIV) But by the grace of God I am what I am, and his grace to me was not without effect. No, I worked harder than all of them—yet not I, but the grace of God that was with me.

Note to self:

____

____

____

____

____

Day 7

<u>Rest</u>

A word we women don't seem to understand. Please take time for yourselves. I know how we are; everything matters more than 'us'. We think about our spouses, our children, our jobs and everything else before we give a thought to ourselves. Today I'm saying, slow down, stop even and rest. Do you need to slip away from it all? Okay, go for it.

Go to your room and close the door, go for a drive if that is what is needed. I'm serious, book into a hotel for a couple of days! Your body is God's temple. Do not neglect to take care of it. It would be a sin for you to continue going, if you know that you are tired and worn down. God loves you and He wants you to take care of you. Everything will be ok when you get back to it. It can wait!

So, go ahead love yourself!

1 Corinthians 16:14 (NIV) Do everything in love.

Note to self:

____

____

____

____

____

Day 8

<u>Don't be Afraid to Dream</u>

It's the dreams that we have that propel us to go forth and spread our wings. Without dreams there is no purpose, no desire to move ahead. So, think about those awesome ideas you've been turning around in your head; why are they still just in your head though? Do something about it. Do the research, call someone and ask some necessary questions.

 Start! If you never start then you will never know what possibilities await you. Don't stifle your dreams and don't be afraid to dream. God gave you those dreams, and He has also given you a choice. You can choose to be complacent or you can choose to become proactive and shoot for the stars. Let today be that day. Go for it!

Genesis 40:8 (NIV) "We both had dreams," they answered, "but there is no one to interpret them." Then Joseph said to them, "Do not interpretations belong to God? Tell me your dreams."

Note to self:

____

____

____

____

____

____

Day 9

It's Okay to Cry

So, you're not feeling so 'hot' today. Is that a crime? No, it isn't! You are human and we have days when it is just not going to go as we've hoped. Let it out; cry, cry loud and hard. Sob and sob until you feel better. Does that make you weak? No, it makes you human. Feel that tender embrace from our Father above as you sink into yourself for a moment.

Let him hold you and release peace back into your inner being. Stay there for a while, then begin to calm those tears, and once again find solace in the strength, He's pouring into you. Hannah wept to God, and what did He do? He heard and answered her. He will answer and comfort you as well!

1 Samuel 1:10 (NIV) In her deep anguish Hannah prayed to the LORD, weeping bitterly.

Note to self:

____

____

____

____

____

Day 10

<u>Gods Got Your Back</u>

God has done so much for me, and now He's doing so much through me. I can't even believe how much of my life I've wasted going my way and doing my own thing. I guess the statement; "The older you get the wiser you become." is true. The past three years have been a serious journey for me, but it has certainly taught me in no 'jokie,' way who God really is. He has drawn me so close unto Himself but that's after I fell face down and cried out to Him.

 I needed purpose and direction, but first I had to submit to Him and allow Him to completely take over, and He has! If that sounds like you today, do it. Fall to your knees and submit your entire self to God, He can and will fix everything!

Job 22:21 (NIV) "Submit to God and be at peace with him; in this way prosperity will come to you."

Note to Self:

____

____

____

____

____

____

Day 11

<u>Conquer those Fears</u>

It is so easy for fear to take charge of us, sending us spiralling into utter darkness. The first thing I need you to know is that fear is not of God! It's a weapon of the enemy, used to trap us into lack of upward mobility. He doesn't want to see you try, he doesn't want to see you happy, and he doesn't want you to succeed! So, he brings fear into your spirit to kill all your plans and dreams.

The devil however, is powerless over God's children. Stand in the face of fear and rebuke it in the mighty name of Jesus Christ of Nazareth! Open your mouth and bind up every power of darkness over your life and your future! You have the power, use it!

Deuteronomy 31:8 (NIV) The LORD himself goes before you and will be with you; he will never leave you nor forsake you. Do not be afraid; do not be discouraged."

Note to self:

____

____

____

____

____

____

Day 12

<u>Delayed not Denied</u>

Why are you crying? Why are you worried? What has gotten you so burdened? Did you tell it to our daddy? Did you call Him and let Him know you have a problem? Girl, you know He is always ready to come to your aid. And if you called and He said wait, then wait! Delay does not mean denied. He knows your every need and He will fulfill every last one, just you wait and see. Dry those tears and begin to rejoice for the bounty that is about to become yours!
Our Father is rich in all things and there is nothing too good for you, so hush your crying and rejoice. You are chosen. You are royal! You are His! Wait! He is an on-time God.
His timing is perfect. With Him everything is planned and executed right on time.

Hebrews 10:37 (NIV) "In just a little while, he who is coming will come and will not delay."

Note to self:

____

____

____

____

____

____

Day 13

Hope in Troubled Times

Is there anyone who can say they have never had troubles? No. Troubles come to everyone's door at some point. Be comforted though that all things are just for a season. Today you may be troubled, but tomorrow you will be rejoicing. I hear someone say, "Trouble may last for a night but joy comes in the morning." Extend your hope and believe that the one who brought you this far will never leave you nor forsake you. You are His. You are His handy work and He will not allow anything to tear you away from His promises. What He says he will do, that he will do. Isaiah 41:10 states clearly his promises and He is not a man, that He should lie. Take comfort in the faithfulness of the God that you serve.

Isaiah 41:10 (NIV) So do not fear, for I am with you; do not be dismayed, for I am your God. I will strengthen you and help you; I will uphold you with my righteous right hand.

Note to Self:

____

____

____

____

____

Day 14

<u>Knitted into Perfection</u>

Have you ever thought about how you were made? When was the last time you looked at yourself naked in the mirror? Maybe you should do it today. Remind yourself of the masterpiece that God created with His very hands. When He looks at you, He sees beauty and class. What do you see? Remind yourself of your beauty, your worth. God knows what He created and how He knitted you perfectly into that body that stands staring you queer in the face.

 Appreciate your curves and your flawlessness. It doesn't matter who don't see or notice, as long as you do. Love yourself as you are and celebrate your uniqueness. God has never created anything or anyone that He hasn't looked at, smiled and said," And it is good!"

Psalm 139:14 (NIV) I praise you because I am fearfully and wonderfully made; your works are wonderful; I know that full well.

Note to Self:

____

____

____

____

____

____

Day 15

God's Favour is Upon You!

Today, God wants you to know that He is watching you. He has His eyes on everything concerning you. He sees your reservation and your reluctance and He wants you to know that you are covered and empowered by His Holy Spirit. Go forth and do the things that you are called to do. You are a leader and a master at your trade. Rise above fear and fly! I am here to call forth the dead dreams that continue to decay in your mind. God has a work for you to do and He wants you to know that you do not have to be afraid anymore, because His favour is upon you.
Rise above your circumstances and give God the glory for what He alone has the power to see. Trust that your destiny is rooted in the powerful plans of God.

Psalm 84:11 (NIV) for the LORD God is a sun and shield; the LORD bestows favor and honor; no good thing does he withhold from those whose walk is blameless.

Note to Self:

____

____

____

____

____

Day 16

<u>Who Can I Trust?</u>

This is a question I believe we have all asked at some point in our lives. Some of us have been betrayed and belittled to a point of almost no return, and we find it just a tad bit difficult to allow other human beings into our personal space. I speak from experience when I say trust does not come easy when you have been at the hurtful end of a stick. Betrayal by those you trust can cause life-long devastating scars.

Never-the-less my sisters, let us open up our hearts to the sweet healing of Christ's undying, uncompromised and incomparable love towards us. We may find it difficult to trust other human beings at this time but if we put our trust in God then He in His time will restore our ability to trust others. God wants to bring healing and restoration to our broken hearts.

Psalm 16:1 (NIV) "Keep me safe, my God, for in you I take refuge."

Note to Self:

____

____

____

____

____

Day 17

<u>Mom, I Need You</u>

I know many of us have been in that place where life and its worries become so overwhelming that our only desire is to call our moms and to retreat to the arms that we know brings safety and security. Isn't it amazing how we never out-grow the desire to call our moms whenever things are not going as planned? We grow up looking to these, 'super humans' to solve every little sign of conflict in our lives and although we grow up, move out and become 'super humans' to some other little people, that desire to call for our moms never changes. At the first sight of trouble, we want our moms. May they be blessed and favoured by God today as we continue to draw strength from their wisdom.

Proverbs 31:28-29 (NIV) Her children arise and call her blessed; her husband also, and he praises her: "Many women do noble things, but you surpass them all."

Note to Self:

____

____

____

____

____

Day 18

<u>Strong</u>

Together we are strong! God has placed us in communities for a reason. We all need one another in some form or the other. No one is completely self sufficient. No matter how educated or how successful you are, I guarantee you that at some point you will need the empowerment of a strong sister!
There are times when we just don't know how to move beyond a situation and we need to call on some trustworthy sisters who will stand around us and proclaim life and healing. Our journey is not one to embark upon alone. It is a shared adventure; one that includes other ladies that have gone through similar circumstances or will at some point and can come alongside us and pray for breakthrough and deliverance.

Romans 12:12-13 (NIV) Be joyful in hope, patient in affliction, faithful in prayer. Share with the Lord's people who are in need. Practice hospitality.

Note to Self:

____

____

____

____

____

Day 19

<u>Faith Makes it all Possible</u>

Faith is believing that the things we've hoped for, will come to pass in its due season. We may not be able to say how these things will happen but we have the assurance that it will. As children of God, we are called to exercise faith in all circumstances. There are times when all around is gloom and we cannot see a glimmer of light, but this is when our faith is truly put to the test. The God of Daniel and of Joseph is our God. He has not changed and He will never change. He is the same yesterday, today and He will be the same tomorrow. Who on earth have we but thee, whom in heaven have we but thee oh Lord? Faith in God makes all things possible.

Hebrews 11:6 (NIV) And without faith it is impossible to please God, because anyone who comes to him must believe that he exists and that he rewards those who earnestly seek him.

Note to Self:

____

____

____

____

____

Day 20

<u>You Won't End Unless You Begin</u>

Is there something you should be doing that you have been avoiding for some reason? Well, if there is, then this is for you. God is beckoning to you to move forward with those plans. Pull out the old, dusty drawing pad and begin to etch in its pages the direction you should be going in; pray and ask God for His guidance as you seek to take this bold step, then go! God is faithful and He will not allow you to do this on your own.
 He will send all the relief you need to get through. God had instructed Elijah to hide in the Kerith Ravine. He did not leave him alone but in His faithfulness and kindness He sent ravens to feed Elijah. The journey begins with a single step that will lead you to the end. Be an Elijah and be obedient to God!

*Proverbs 16:3 (NIV) Commit to the LORD whatever you do,
and he will establish your plans.*

Note to self:

____

____

____

____

____

____

Day 21

<u>Pray with Your Heart Open</u>

I know that as women of God we know how to pray. It is through prayer that we storm heaven for the things we need for ourselves and our families. We stand in the gap for everyone and everything, but I know sometimes it can seem like a request is taking longer than usual to be answered. We labour and labour and it just feels like nothing is happening. Sometimes it's almost as if our prayers are bouncing back at us. Many times, the problem is us.

Our hearts are not opened for God to enter. God is unique and he wants to come in. He has no pleasure talking to us from the outer banks. So, today when you call, remember to open up to Him as well. Give Him full access to not just solve a problem but to heal a soul.

Acts 2:21 (NIV) And everyone who calls on the name of the Lord will be saved.'

Note to Self:

____

____

____

____

____

Day 22

<u>Fancy Shoes</u>

So, as I think about this topic, I'm smiling from ear to ear just because, I like fancy shoes. Yes, I do! I will not pretend for you; I like nice things. I believe that when I step out, I must look good. You must look good too. You work hard, don't you? Yeah, so why should you look 'shabby,' when you leave your house? Listen, you are a child of God.

You must look better than the world! So, if going out and buying yourself nice things make you happy, then go ahead, do it! I am not saying be impulsive, I'm saying plan your thing, and take care of your needs. The scripture below says that your body is His temple, so go ahead and make it look good, just guard your heart and don't allow vanity to creep in.

1 Corinthians 3:16 (NIV) Don't you know that you yourselves are God's temple and that God's Spirit dwells in your midst?

Note to Self:

____

____

____

____

____

____

Day 23

<u>Find your Voice</u>

We are sometimes silenced by the powers over and around us, but that is not God's plans for you my sister, no it isn't. You are precious to Him and He wants to hear your voice. If He wanted you silenced, then He would not have made you to speak.
So today I want you to think about all the situations that rock your boat.
Is there someone or something that is preventing you from speaking up? If there is, today is the day to find that inner strength that God has equipped you with. Pray and seek His face, give yourself time to hear from him and then go ahead; speak, speak loud and clear!

2 Kings 4:9-10 (NIV) She said to her husband, "I know that this man who often comes our way is a holy man of God. Let's make a small room on the roof and put in it a bed and a table, a chair and a lamp for him. Then he can stay there whenever he comes to us."

Note to Self:

____

____

____

____

____

Day 24

<u>Are We There Yet?</u>

We sometimes get anxious about how long things are taking to materialize. We are humans after all and so we want to see things happening, sometimes just a little faster that it should. It's wonderful that God loves us so much that He refuses to give us things pre-maturely, knowing full well if that happened it would totally destroy some of us.

I am so happy that I have a Father who knows me so well and knows how to release things to me slowly and cautiously so that I don't utterly and completely wreck myself with the gifts that were meant for good and not for evil. So, are we there yet? Maybe not! Keep on waiting with lots of praises and expectations.

Psalm 62:5 (NIV) Yes, my soul, find rest in God;
my hope comes from him.

Note to Self:

____

____

____

____

____

____

Day 25

Hopeful & Happy

Never lose hope, for if you do all is lost! Having hope is expecting
that something is going to happen though you don't know how,
or when. I want you to have hope, while also remaining happy.
Don't allow the situation to weigh you down so much that you
forget to smile, laugh, call your family and friends, or go out for
coffee. Yes, live, live in hope that things will not remain as they
are. That means being happy throughout the process.
Give God thanks for what He has already done and for what He's
going to do, believing without seeing, but knowing that in time
all things will fall into its rightful place. Is He a man that He
should lie? No, He isn't, so trust the process and be joyful
knowing that all testing comes to give us a great testimony.

*Hebrews 10:23 (NIV) Let us hold unswervingly to the hope we profess,
for he who promised is faithful.*

Note to Self:

____

____

____

____

____

Day 26

<u>Smile in Spite of the Tears</u>

I know that it is hard to smile when it seems like all the world's troubles have somehow fallen on your shoulders and there is no one to help you carry that load. Often, it appears that before one struggle is over another one begins. We reach out to God asking, 'Why Lord, why me?' Isn't it amazing that this seem to be the time He goes quiet on us? Yeah, it is and that makes us angry and frustrated. But, let me remind you of what one writer says, "When you saw only on set of foot prints in the sand, it was then that I was carrying you."
 He may seem quiet in the midst of your struggles but He never sleeps nor slumbers. He is always taking care of you! So, rest assured today that when you see only one set of footprints in the sand that is when He is carrying you.

Isaiah 41:10 (NIV) So do not fear, for I am with you;
do not be dismayed, for I am your God. I will strengthen you and help you;
I will uphold you with my righteous right hand.

Note to Self:

____

____

____

____

____

Day 27

<u>Encourage Others</u>

God has called us to love and encourage one another. I know we all have different struggles and concerns in our lives, but as Christians God wants us to fill our lives with the things that concern His people. We are expected to spend quality time checking on God's children, finding out what their needs and struggles are and how we can help with easing their troubles. He has promised that when we make His business a priority then He will make us His priority. So today, don't worry so much about you, rather replace those thoughts with whomever God has placed upon your heart to love and encourage today.

Romans 15:5 (NIV) May the God who gives endurance and encouragement give you the same attitude of mind toward each other that Christ Jesus had.

Note to Self:

____

____

____

____

____

Day 28

<u>Yes Sir, Right Away</u>

I think about this topic and my heart goes out to the many sisters out there who are oppressed, suppressed and depressed because of what they are facing in their work places. Every day you get up, get dressed and put your best self forward, knowing that your worth is not even observed, but you do it anyway. You respectfully approach your work with the professionalism that is your standard and you do it day after day because that is who you are. Well, today I salute you and I say God loves you and He sees your sacrifice and He will reward you openly. Just have faith and trust His timing! He will never give you more than you can bear. When the time is right, if that is His plan for you, you will get the recognition you deserve or He will simply remove you from the toxic environment and place you where you can thrive.

Numbers 6:24-26 (NIV) "The LORD bless you and keep you;
the LORD makes his face shine on you and be gracious to you;
the LORD turns his face toward you and give you peace."

Note to Self:

____

____

____

____

____

Day 29

Make a Habit of It

You know we often hear that; God inhabits the praises of His people. Well, I have proven that to be so true. I have been on a serious journey with God where I couldn't understand a lot of things that was going on in my life or rather; not going on in life and I was just praying and asking lots of questions that I felt I wasn't even getting answers to.

I remember Him sending me at different times to listen to T.D. Jakes and Joel Osteen and it was always as if they were speaking directly into me. It was the wisdom of those men that opened my eyes to making praises a habit and allowing God to do what only He could do. And can I tell you this, it's amazing! Try it, make praises a habit and watch God transform and shatter your norm.

Psalms 22:3 (KJV) But thou art holy, O thou that inhabits the praises of Israel.

Note to Self:

____

____

____

____

____

Day 30

Woman of Substance

A woman who has great influence is one whom we can call a woman of substance. It is one of the greatest honours that can be pronounced upon a person. It means that she put others above herself, and seeks to motivate and elevate them above the norm that the world would suggest they conform to. She seeks to sew into others the elements of truth, forgiveness and purpose, giving them the necessary tools to go forth and make a difference in a world that is warped and needs God's truth.

This is a woman who is not afraid to diminish while her subjects increase. It is not about her; it is about them and God has given her the humility to carry out His master plan to penetrate and empower the lives of those broken and in need of direction and love. This is what God wants all of us to become.

Proverbs 31:26 (NIV) She speaks with wisdom, and faithful instruction is on her tongue.

Note to Self:

____

____

____

____

____

Day 31

<u>Who Cares About Age?</u>

So, you are a year older, is that a crime? Some of us ladies tend to start feeling a bit overwhelmed when we touch that glorious year of 40. Yes, I'm speaking about myself! I have been battling that feeling of, "Oh my God, I'm old!" And to be truly honest, I have not been able to shake it off. It is hard! I feel like these golden years just crept upon me and I wasn't ready. I'm still not ready but I'm praying about it. God will have to give me the help to get through this one. So, if that's how you are feeling too, well, you are not alone sister! Who cares about age? We do, but the scripture below brings peace.
I take comfort in this verse as it promotes what is positive and noteworthy about becoming older. It is truly not a death sentence, quite the contrary.

> *Job 12:12 (NIV) Is not wisdom found among the aged?*
> *Does not long-life bring understanding?*

Note to Self:

____

____

____

____

____

Day 32

<u>Don't Just Hope, Work for it!</u>

Just having the expectation for something to happen is not
enough ladies. With that hope, you must plan out your direction
and begin to aim for where you want to go. You must work on it.
Decide what it is you want to do, and then set time frames. And
don't neglect to write all of this down.
I've come to realize that when I actually write things down, they
become more realistic to me and I can actually see the change as it
is happening, and this encourages me to keep on going. No one is
telling you that there won't be obstacles, of course there will be,
but faith will encourage your work and hope will inspire your
endurance. Keep on going!

*1 Thessalonians 1:3 (NIV) We remember before our God and
Father your work produced by faith, your labour prompted by love,
and your endurance inspired by hope in our Lord Jesus Christ.*

Note to Self:

____

____

____

____

____

____

Day 33

<u>Dreams Demand Doing</u>

Pharaoh had a dream and he knew it had significant meaning, but no one in his kingdom was able to interpret his dreams so he sent for Joseph to tell him what his dreams meant. Joseph did not only explain Pharaoh's dreams to him but he also told him what he needed to do. Had Pharaoh not listened to Joseph's advice, all of Egypt would have starved during the time of the famine.
It's great to have a dream but be wise in ensuring that what is necessary to be done in order to see your dreams become a reality is being done. Anyone can dream but it takes motivation and courage to put the wheels in motion and go for the prize.

Genesis 41:34&36 (NIV) Let Pharaoh appoint commissioners over the land to take a fifth of the harvest of Egypt during the seven years of abundance. This food should be held in reserve for the country, to be used during the seven years of famine that will come upon Egypt, so that the country may not be ruined by the famine.

Note to Self:

____

____

____

____

____

Day 34

<u>Daring & Determined</u>

I know that nothing is going to keep you from reaching your goals. You are a person of action. You know what your goals are and you will stop at nothing to conquer any obstacles that try to get in your way. Your adventurous nature is of great value and it helps to take hesitation and procrastination away. Your determination is worth admiring. **Go for it!** What can stop you from getting to the prize when God is your strength and your vindicator? You are a world class woman who is tenacious and persistent. There is nothing that can hinder you, so go and be blessed and then be a blessing to others. The gifts that God have given to us were not meant for us and us alone. His intention was that we would use our gifts and talents to lift others up.

2 Timothy 4:7 (NIV) I have fought a good fight, I have finished my course, I have kept the faith.

Note to Self:

____

____

____

____

____

____

Day 35

<u>Dare to be Different</u>

Don't allow anyone to tell you that you need to be 'normal,' or that you should do what everybody else is doing. God himself said that we should be in the world but not of this world, so 'dare to be different!' Wear what you like, as long as it is appropriate, speak what is on your mind, as long as it is respectful, and yes, go for that out of this world awesome job that is being advertised on the cooperate front!
If you feel led, then do not allow anyone or anything to stop you from going after your dreams. It doesn't matter how impossible it may seem. If God is for you, then who can be against you?

Romans 8:31 (NIV) What, then, shall we then say in response to these things? If God is for us, who can be against us?

Note to Self:

____

____

____

____

____

Day 36

<u>Who Said You Couldn't?</u>

So, there you go. You have completed that task. I know it wasn't easy and I know that many days you thought you just would not make it to this point, but here you are, finished and accomplished! No important task is ever going to be, 'a walk in the park.' But, if you are serious and if you know who your heavenly Father is, then there is no task that is impossible to conquer. It's all about our faith, faithfulness and favour.
 God has not called us to be timid and fearful. He has placed within us a spirit of hope and perseverance. Celebrate, for you have worked without ceasing, and now your reward is great!

Psalm 90:17 (KJV) And let the beauty of the LORD our God be upon us: and establish thou the work of our hands upon us; yea, the work of our hands establish thou it.

Note to Self:

____

____

____

____

____

Day 37

<u>Vibrant & Vivacious</u>

You are of great value and worth to both your family and your job. You are vibrant and vivacious and you bring life to the party. Nothing is the same when you are not around. Think for a moment about the role you play as mom, wife and that position you hold at work. How exactly would they truly manage without you in that role?

No one can be just like you. That is the gift God has given to you and He wants you to use it daily to build and encourage those around you. So, be your vibrant self. It is what makes you unique and special. Your positive outlook on things helps others to take a second look. Your views are valid and they shed a light that would otherwise go unseen.

Galatians 4:18 (NIV) It is fine to be zealous, provided the purpose is good, and to be so always, not just when I am with you.

Note to Self:

____

____

____

____

____

Day 38

<u>Sunflower Girl</u>

Have you ever seen a real sunflower bloom? I have and that is how I look at you. Today as I write, I'm thinking of all my sisters out there, you, and you and you. Yes, if you are reading this book then yes, I am talking to you! Your radiance is like a beautiful sunflower opened as wide as the sun. God is the soil, the water and the sunshine that nurtured you to this full bloom.

So, stand tall and proud, hold your head up high like a beautiful sunflower and walk like you're a daughter of a king, for that is who you are. Be confident that you have a heritage and that heritage is found in Christ alone.

Psalm 135:12 (NIV) and he gave their land as an inheritance, an inheritance to his people Israel.

Note to Self:

____

____

____

____

____

Day 39

Inspired to Inspire

When was the last time you thought about how your life have been touched and inspired by others? I can think of some beautiful women who have been my strength, my peace and my anchor. God has blessed me with a bouquet of petals that never seem to lose its radiance. My bouquet keeps getting more and more luscious with each passing year. In fact, I'm beginning to notice that this bouquet is getting bigger and more varied than before. I continue to ask God what I have done to deserve such an awesome inspiring gift of love.

These women have prayed for me, directed me, corrected me, cried with me and some have even downright told me off when it was necessary. We all need the blessing of inspiration, and then it's our duty to become someone else's inspiration. Be an inspiration to another woman today.

Hebrews 10:24 (NIV) And let us consider how we may spur one another on toward love and good deeds.

Note to Self:

____

____

____

____

____

Day 40

<u>Knock them Out!</u>

Show them what you are made of. You are educated and intelligent and you are as competent as anyone else there. Are you one of those women who are struggling to prove yourself in your career path? I know it's difficult to compete at times. I know there are times when you just want to walk away and call it a day, but don't quit. The material from which you are made is much stronger than that. You are sewn together with the love and strength of God.

This battle is not yours, its God's. All He wants you to do is show up each day and He will do the rest. That position was created for you by God and no ordinary man can remove you, so go ahead, 'knock them out!'

2 Chronicles 20:15 (NIV) He said: "Listen, King Jehoshaphat and all who live in Judah and Jerusalem! This is what the LORD says to you: 'Do not be afraid or discouraged because of this vast army. For the battle is not yours, but God's.

Note to Self:

____

____

____

____

____

Day 41

<u>Just Believe</u>

So, God have been there all this time, telling you just how much He loves you. How much He is blessing every single thing you touch. He wants you to stop for a moment and notice Him there. He has been trying so hard to call out to you, touch you, to share a moment with you. God wants you to know that He has seen your faithfulness throughout your childhood and teenage years. He sees the awesome wife and mom you have become.

He also sees the pain you have been carrying around from all those years ago. He sees that feeling of lost and rejection that is keeping you from believing in who you are and whose you are. He wants you to know that you are a, 'power tower!' He is saying, 'Let go, and let me!' Give God the chance to heal every scar and mend your broken spirit.

Matthew 21:22 (NIV) If you believe, you will receive whatever you ask for in prayer."

Note to Self:

____

____

____

____

____

Day 42

<u>Watch your Appearance</u>

As women of God, we must choose how our lives will minister to others. What impressions are we giving by our appearances? Do we seem angry and unapproachable or are we pleasant and welcoming? Our very lives are ministries for the kingdom of God so I call you today to be mindful of what you 'sell' to others.

We will all have to give an account for how we affected lives in His church, whether by the way we dress or by how we allow others to feel when approaching us. Be mindful of your part in this Christian walk. If you are called, then you have a part to play. You are beautiful so let that beauty spread to others.

1 Peter 3:3-4 (NIV) Your beauty should not come from outward adornment, such as elaborate hairstyles and the wearing of gold jewellery or fine clothes. Rather, it should be that of your inner self, the unfading beauty of a gentle and quiet spirit, which is of great worth in God's sight.

Note to self:

____

____

____

____

____

____

Day 43

<u>Battered but not Broken</u>

The unexpected events of life do come. It's never a matter of, if they will come but when. We are sometimes hit from an unexpected angle; illness, lost of employment or the sudden lost of a loved one. These events can drive a devastating blow to a person, leaving them paralyzed mentally. Although in times like these we want to believe that God is still near, it can be very hard and sometimes completely impossible in one's mind.

How can someone in excruciating pain experience any resemblance of peace? Only through God's grace! We are reminded in the scripture below that we may be struck down but we are not destroyed. So, turn to Him and He will heal your brokenness.

> *2 Corinthians 4:8-9 (NIV) We are hard pressed on every side, but not crushed; perplexed, but not in despair; persecuted, but not abandoned; struck down, but not destroyed.*

Note to Self:

____

____

____

____

____

Day 44

Friends for Life

There are people who come into our lives for a reason and sometimes for a season. Some people are definitely not here to stay and you have to be quite mindful of how much you allow them to know about you, but then there are those rare gems that enter your space and they have come to enlighten, encourage, support and love you through all of life's ups and downs.

 They are there with no other interest but to help you in every way to be the best version of you that you can possibly be. They laugh with you, talk with you about everything from the smallest to the greatest of detail, they plan with you, cry with you when they need to, and expect with you for all that life has to offer. They are your forever friends! Cherish them and let them know how much they mean to you.

Proverbs 18:24 (NLT) There are "friends" who destroy each other, but a real friend sticks closer than a brother.

Note to Self:

____

____

____

____

____

____

Day 45

<u>Chocolate & Ice Cream</u>

Chocolate and ice cream are two of my favourite things. Agreed, it's not good to have these delicious treats every day, but ever so often it's okay to treat yourself. We sometimes get so wrapped up in how we look that we forbid ourselves to eat every, and anything that is yummy and enjoyable. Don't get me wrong all my health-conscious sisters, I am weight conscious too, but cut your selves some slacks. We work hard, don't we?
Yes, we do! So, set that time aside for playing. Go out with a few friends and indulge, allow yourself a well-deserved treat or two. We are always our greatest critique, and we come down hard on ourselves, but everything has its place and its time. Today take a break from the rigid routine and take care of those inner cries to break loose a little.

Ecclesiastes 3:13 (NIV) That each of them may eat and drink, and find satisfaction in all their toil—this is the gift of God.

Note to Self:

____

____

____

____

____

____

Day 46

May your Faith be Stronger than your Feelings

Let's be honest, we ladies have a way of allowing our feelings to run out of control. Uh hum! You know it's true, I know it's true and our husbands know its true (laugh). I know it's hard to control those emotions but we need to! We can't allow everything we feel to twist and turn us into someone that no one can recognize.

God has given us a spirit of power and of love and of a sound mind. We can use that gift so that we are a blessing to ourselves and all those around us. My hope and prayer are that your faith will over shadow your feelings and that you will have complete power over your emotions. Do not allow your feelings to determine how you behave today. Remember that feelings are temporary; don't give them control!

2 Timothy 1:7 (KJV) For God hath not given us the spirit of fear; but of power, and of love, and of a sound mind.

Note to Self:

____

____

____

____

____

Day 47

<u>Grateful for Connections</u>

It's truly amazing how God can take complete strangers and strategically place them in your life to bless you beyond anything you could ever think or even imagine. I am at a place in my life where I am so completely and utterly grateful to God for the connections, He has seen fit to give unto me; not because I deserve them but because He loves me so much!

There are some people that surround my family and I and I cannot imagine my life without them in it anymore. They have become our towers of strength, peace, love and everything else! Some days I have to say Lord, who am I that you God think it necessary to bring such blessings into my life? It's amazing!

See your connections as blessings and give God thanks for them.

1 Thessalonians 1:2 (KJV) We give thanks to God always for you all, making mention of you in our prayers.

Note to Self:

____

____

____

____

____

____

Day 48

Take a Stand

Taking a stand, when you are the only one standing can be a super difficult thing to do. But God has not given us a spirit of fear. In fact, if we truly believe something is wrong then it is our duty to take a stand. We must first pray and seek God's direction in every situation. When we are certain that we have heard from Him then we can act accordingly.

Sometimes it's something as simple as an argument between husband and wife, parent and child or a little trickier; a situation at work. Whatever the situation is however, God does not want us to live a miserable life. He wants us to be happy, so take the stands you need to with God as your main sail, the direction beneath your wings.

Psalm 32:8 (NIV) I will instruct you and teach you in the way you should go;
I will counsel you with my loving eye on you.

Note to Self:

____

____

____

____

____

____

Day 49

<u>Soul Search</u>

How often do you 'soul search'? Maybe every now and then or maybe you have never done this activity. Whichever way, soul searching is a very important thing to do. It is simply stepping back and giving yourself some space and time to think about, reflect on your life and the things that matters the most to you. It's taking the time to evaluate if things have been going according to your plans and desires.

Find a quiet place to engage in this activity, away from distractions and interruptions, where you can fully focus and allow yourself to go deep into your soul. Ensure that as you begin, you invite God's presence into your quiet space as you will need Him to guide you through where you have been and indeed where you need to go.

Lamentations 3:25 (NIV) The LORD is good to those whose hope is in him, to the one who seeks him.

Note to Self:

____

____

____

____

____

____

Day 50

<u>Do I Still Love Him?</u>

If we are truly honest, this is a question many of us ask ourselves from time to time. If you have never done it, well, hats off to you! The fact of the matter is that sometimes our husbands drive the 'bolts off our nuts!' They can send us spiralling downstream in split seconds if we are not careful. So, yeah, the occasional question does come.

Let's be fair though, we can drive them a bit, 'ballistic' sometimes as well. Listen, God didn't make us or them perfect, but He made us compatible. We are different and unique but we complement each other. Things will not always be smooth sailing, but that reminds us that we are all imperfect beings living in an imperfect world. Love your spouse and try to see the best in all that God has given you!

Roman 11:36 (NIV) For from him and through him and for him are all things. To him be the glory forever! Amen.

Note to Self:

____

____

____

____

____

Day 51

<u>It is not your Job to Change Him</u>

I hear you. He is overbearing, selfish, inconsiderate, and when
was the last time he bought you a special gift for no reason? I hear
your heart sister and I feel your pain, but just for a moment I want
you to look back to when you just met. Do you remember how he
larded over you, telling you the sweetest things in your ear,
buying you the most expensive gifts?
Yes, that's the same man you have today. Things have changed.
Responsibilities have been added, time is now shared, so don't be
so hard on him. And if he has changed, then pray and allow God
to do His work in him. Your job is to love him no matter what!
Well isn't that what you vowed before God and man? Uh huh!
God sees your tears and your fears so pray, pray, pray and allow
God to do His perfect work both in you and in that man that you
love.

*Proverbs 21:2 (NIV) A person may think their own ways are right,
but the LORD weighs the heart.*

Note to Self:

____

____

____

____

____

51

Day 52

<u>Work on You</u>

It's never easy to be the bigger man and walk away from an argument, especially when you know you are right. Right can be relative however. There are times when we must simply step back and allow God to go to work where we have no power. Ladies, listen, I'm speaking to you as much as I am speaking to myself. We cannot and should not want to change our husbands or our kids for that matter.

I pray instead, that we would spend more time in prayer seeking Gods face and giving him the power to change us so that through our willing transformation, we would be surprised by the things that happen in the lives of those around us. When we focus on ourselves and God, He will bring all things concerning us into direct vision!

Lamentations 3:40 (NIV) Let us examine our ways and test them, and let us return to the LORD.

Note to Self:

____

____

____

____

____

Day 53

<u>God Made Him the Head</u>

Throughout the ages we have seen men taking on the role as leaders, as the head of the household, the church, government and definitely the Bible says they are the head of the wife. This sometimes is not what we want to hear. Speaking from experience, I have rebelled against this notion for as long as I can remember. My thought was always, I'm independent and strong and I don't want anyone telling me what to do, when or how! But, if we are to live in the will of our Lord and Saviour then yes, we must conform to His commands.

They are the head and we are there to love and support them, to be their help mate. I know things have changed and now we are doing as much as men and sometimes even more, but let us remain humble and live in God's will so that His blessings will flow over us and our families.

Ephesians 5:23 (NIV) for the husband is the head of the wife as Christ is the head of the church, his body, of which he is the Savior.

Note to Self:

____

____

____

____

Day 54

<u>Be His Helpmate</u>

A helpmate is a helpful companion or partner, especially one's husband or wife. This is who God has called us to be; a helpmate for our husbands. I know it is sometimes very difficult, especially when the husbands aren't living up to expectations regarding their responsibilities. But can I tell you something? If you do what God has called you to do as a wife, that is, to love these men in their imperfections, then God out of His love and compassion for you will do the rest. He sees every tear and hears every heart's cry. He loves you enough to send His only son to die for you and for me. Do you think He will allow you to suffer beyond what you can bear if you are living in His will? No, He will not! In the beginning God said it was not good for man to be alone. They need us!

Genesis 2:18 (NIV) The LORD God said, "It is not good for the man to be alone. I will make a helper suitable for him."

Note to Self:

____

____

____

____

____

Day 55

<u>A Bouquet of Kindness</u>

Today I received a beautiful bouquet from a lady who has become
a very dear friend. It reminded me that there are still kind,
thoughtful people out there; people who want nothing in return,
but simply takes pleasure in making others feel appreciated and
loved. God has called us to show love one to another regardless of
colour, class or creed.
May we find it in our hearts today to reach out to someone; a
sister, a friend or even a neighbour who might be on your mind.
There are people out there who are lonely, sad and broken and
could use a call, a coffee date or just a surprise bouquet that
reminds them that there is someone, somewhere who cares.

*Galatians 6:10 (NIV) Therefore, as we have opportunity,
let us do good to all people, especially to those who
belong to the family of believers.*

Note to Self:

____

____

____

____

____

Day 56

<u>Save the Date</u>

It is very important to find time to build strong meaningful relationships with other women. God did not mean for us to do life by ourselves. We are social beings and we all need other people to lean on, to speak into our lives and to encourage us when times get rough. Call up a few friends and make it a date to spend some time together. Talk about the things that are going great in your lives and then pray together about those things that are not going according to your plans and expectations. When Godly women come together to pray barriers and chains are miraculously broken. Trust God and thank him for those God-fearing women in your lives. Find the time to meet together, agree together and watch God align things as they should be.

1 Thessalonians 5:11 (NIV) Therefore encourage one another an build each other up, just as in fact you are doing.

Note to Self:

____

____

____

____

____

____

Day 57

<u>Gathered Around the Fire</u>

There is something so beautiful about a set of awesome ladies gathered together around a fireplace or in the backyard. I had the opportunity to do this with some co-workers and it was amazing. I began working with these lovely ladies almost a year ago and already they are like family. They immediately welcomed me in and I felt right at home in their midst.

Our Dress Club has become an exciting monthly expectation and we look forward to our time together. It is important to have people in your life, and events like these, scheduled regularly as they give us a sense of belonging and purpose. Something to look forward to and then a time to sit in similar company, kick back and rejuvenate!

Psalm 103 1a& 5 (NIV) Praise the Lord…who satisfies your desires with good things so that your youth is renewed like the eagle's.

Note to Self:

____

____

____

____

____

____

Day 58

<u>Faithful in Disappointments</u>

If there is one thing I know, it's that we women are strong. We know how to overcome the worst of circumstances and still shine. Life has a way of throwing fiery darts at us in all aspects of our lives. Still we remain faithful and carry on as if nothing is happening. Sometimes it is in our marriages, in our workplaces, or in very personal family relationships.

However, we are so good at hiding our emotions that if we don't tell someone what we are going through they would never know. We know how to get up each day and put ourselves together and move forward in faith and hope that God will show up right on time. If you are going through this today be reminded that you are not alone. God's got you! Remain faithful and fight your battles on your knees!

James 4:10 (MSG) Get down on your knees before the Master; it's the only way you'll get on your feet.

Note to Self:

____

____

____

____

____

____

Day 59

<u>We Don't Judge; we Journey with…</u>

It's not uncommon for some women to be very reserved or cautious, introverted even. I know I am! We are not comfortable with speaking to just anyone or everyone, to release any form of information about ourselves no matter how simple or insignificant it may seem. We are always in a 'fight or flight' kind of mindset. It is unfortunate, and in some ways very sad, as God did not intend for us to do life alone. However, because of past experiences with hurt and disappointments from those we may have trusted, we resort to withdrawing into ourselves. I want you to know today that it is ok to open up and trust again. It is what God wants you to do. Find a few good ladies whose motive is to journey with you not to judge you, and then work on developing lasting, trusting relationships. Yes, they do exist and I should know because I have a few "ride or dies," that I can truly count on and I thank God for them every single day.

James 3:17 (NIV) But the wisdom that comes from heaven is first of all pure; then peace-loving, considerate, submissive, full of mercy and good fruit, impartial and sincere.

Note to Self:

____

____

____

____

____

Day 60

<u>Don't Lose Your Culture</u>

We live in a rather diversified world. Yet, if you don't fit into a particular racial ethnicity you are seen, unfortunately, as inferior. Don't allow this to deter you. We all originated from Adam's linage, but God has diversified His people and we must learn to love and appreciate the beauty He has created in all people no matter their culture, colour of their skin or their intellectual capacity. What an absolutely boring world it would be if we had the same cultural background! I am from a Jamaican culture where when our Reggae music 'hits we feel no pain.' Yet I live in Canada and my family has fully embraced much of Canada's culture and we respect and love it, as well as the wonderful people who originated here or simply has come from all over the world with their diverse culture and has made this lovely country an even more beautiful and breathtaking place to call home. So, embrace your culture and never lose your identity!

Romans 12:2 (NIV) Do not conform to the pattern of this world, but be transformed by the renewing of your mind. Then you will able to test and approve what God's will is—his good, pleasing and perfect will.

Note to Self:

____

____

____

____

Day 61

What Defines who you Are?

A very thought-provoking question, isn't it? Well it should be, and that is exactly why I am asking it. Who are you? When was the last time you took a moment to examine yourself from the inside out? So maybe you have moved away from your home town and you are now living in a place that is completely different from where you grew up. That's fine, that's totally okay. But how has that altered who you are?

Have you forgotten what your parents took the time to instil in you? Have you walked away from the morals and values of the local church? Or are you exemplifying Gods truth in who you are and how you choose to live? Remember to be set apart, be yourself and never forget who God has called you to be.

Psalm 4:3 (NIV) Know that the LORD has set apart his faithful servant for himself; the LORD hears when I call to him.

Note to Self:

____

____

____

____

____

Day 62

Let go of What Was!

You have been in that place for far too long. It's time to get up and get moving! Why are you allowing life to pass you by while you sulk and cry about what was? God is all knowing and all powerful, and if He in His wisdom has chosen to pull you out of that situation, why are you still living in the memories of what was? My sister, God said to get up and get moving! You may feel like you have lost so much but can I tell you this; you have lost nothing! What God has saved you from is nothing short of a miracle and what He has in store for you is nothing short of a blessing! So, get over it, get up and get moving! God is waiting on you. He is ready for you to let go of what was, and boldly step into what He has prepared for you!

Isaiah 43:18-19 (NIV) "Forget the former things; do not dwell on the past.
See, I am doing a new thing! Now it springs up; do you not perceive it?
I am making a way in the wilderness and streams in the wasteland.

Note to Self:

____

____

____

____

____

____

Day 63

<u>Your Yesterday is Foundation for Your Tomorrow</u>

Stop regretting, God has not done anything that He did not mean to do. So, stop regretting! Our God does not make mistakes. He is a perfect God! He is awesome, He is wonderful, He is gracious and what you have been through is foundation for what He's about to build in and through you! God's plans are unique and they are incomprehensible to the human mind. We cannot fathom who God is, what He does or why He does them. We are called to just have faith in Him. Rejoice in the face of adversities. Shout and praise God when it seems all around is sinking sand for if you know God, then you know that he's coming like a roaring lion to devour anyone and any situation that is causing His children pain and suffering. Set yourself right with God and know that everything you are going through only came to make you stronger.

Psalm 51:10 (NIV) Create in me a pure heart, O God,
and renew a steadfast spirit within me.

Note to Self:

____

____

____

____

____

Day 64

Shine for Her

Our daughters are a gift to us from God and we must live a life that exemplifies God's love and truth for them to see and emulate. You may not think they are watching but don't be mistaken. Allow yourself to take the time to observe their daily behaviours; their walk, their words, the type of clothes they want to wear. Are they putting on lipstick, nail polish and makeup?

Uh huh, of course they are. That's what they see you do. They are slowly but surely becoming a 'mini you.' So, be mindful of what you are silently teaching her. Ensure that what is passed on is positive, wholesome and most of all Godly!

Proverbs 22:6 (NIV) Start children off on the way they should go, and even when they are old, they will not turn from it.

Note to Self:

____

____

____

____

____

Day 65

<u>The Soccer Mom</u>

It's not just her that's watching you, he is too. Yes, you are a mom of both girls and boys and they are both learning from you. He's learning what it is to be a loving, dedicated woman. One who loves her husband and her kids and looks out for their best interest every single day. You're giving him a pre-view of what a good wife, 'looks like.' He will use who you are to determine if a woman is a good fit for him. Exemplify those qualities you would love for him to find in his future wife and you would have helped to choose a good life long partner for him without even saying a word. He sees all your sacrifices and support and it's building his character. It will help him to become a strong, loving, respectful, dedicated God-fearing man.

Proverbs 31:28 (NKJV) Her children rise up and call her blessed; Her husband also, and he praises her

Note to Self:

____

____

____

____

____

Day 66

A Picturesque Scene

It's amazing how we can live in the same place for years and not know what's around us. We don't stop to enjoy the beauty and the tranquility. They are there just for our enjoyment and rejuvenation. A few days ago, a friend of mine invited me to what she had come to love as her own 'special place.' It was breath taking and I couldn't believe I had lived here for so long and had never seen this place or was even aware that it existed. The tall trees and the river that runs by are so beautiful. I felt one with nature and was just basking in the beautiful creation that God had strategically put in this place for His children to enjoy. I felt just like a little bit of heaven was right there in that place and for sure I will be going back to share it with my family and other friends as well. It is something to share and thankfully my friend felt the desire to share it with me. I'm so grateful! What do you need to slow down and enjoy today?

Matthew 6:29 (ESV) Yet I tell you, even Solomon in all his glory was not arrayed like one of these.

Note to Self:

____

____

____

____

Day 67

<u>My Soaker Tub</u>

A soaker tub may seem like a simple thing for some people and for others, not even necessary. For me however, it is a priceless commodity. It is simply something I love. Life is short, and sometimes we lose sight of the simple but treasured things we have access to right in our own environment. We often think we need to go to a faraway place on a vacation, or we have to save for five years in order to relax, have fun and live! That however is so far from the truth. I have been there but, I am learning that it is the here and now that matters the most. Don't get me wrong, vacations are great and I love them but I'm encouraging you to take another look at that soaker tub today, transform it into your own bit of heaven, your escape, right there in your home, and enjoy the here and now. Take some time to appreciate what you do have, relax and enjoy.

Ephesians 5:15-16 (ESV) Look carefully then how you walk, not as unwise but as wise, making the best use of the time, because the days are evil.

Note to Self:

____

____

____

____

____

____

Day 68

The Smell of Fragrance

Some persons have a great love for fragrances, like me, and some persons don't for one reason or another. Some persons have allergies and that is quite understandable. I love to use different fragrant in my home because I love that sweet fresh scent when I open my door. I believe your home should be a place that is warm and welcoming and scents do that for me. The question is, what does it for you, what gives you that feeling? If its scents like me, then use them to give that extra tinkle in the air. If it's something else that's ok too, find it and use it to your advantage. The aim is to make your home a place of comfort, a place you can get excited to go especially after a hard day at work. Kids need this as well. Make that extra effort to make your home special, for everyone.

Proverbs 24:3-4 (ESV) By wisdom a house is built, and by understanding it is established; by knowledge the rooms are filled with all precious and pleasant riches.

Note to Self:

____

____

____

____

____

Day 69

Dealing with the Unexpected

Things do not always happen as we expect. In fact, often times, the things that actually happen are totally unexpected. On a normal day, like any other day or so I thought, my dad left home to fetch water, never to return. What happened? A heart attack did. Was that expected? No, it wasn't but that was his fate. That is a day forever etched in my mind and soul and nothing will ever change that. The question is, how do you get pass it and move beyond it? That my friend, is a work for the master creator. He gives and He takes away. Unless we are able to make peace with that one fact, we will never be able to get pass the unexpected blows of this life. It may have been the loss of a child, a miscarriage, the loss of a job. No matter what it is, only He has the power to move us beyond the hurt and the pain to healing and restoration.

Jeremiah 17:14 (ESV) Heal me, O LORD, and I shall be healed; save me, and I shall be saved, for you are my praise.

Note to Self:

____

____

____

____

____

Day 70

<u>Roses & Tulips</u>

Roses and tulips are two of my favourite flowers. They are similar to me but also different. They both are beautiful flowers that can be used in different capacities. I got married holding roses but my program had tulips on them. They worked together and made my day even more special and beautiful. We have lots of roses and tulips in this world. It doesn't matter if you are round and fluffy like a rose or if you are straight and tall like a tulip. The important thing is the role you play from day to day and how you see or feel about yourself. You are beautiful the way God made you and He has made you for a purpose. Serve your purpose and do it with precision and pride.

Ephesians 2:10 (NIV) For we are God's handiwork, created in Christ Jesus to do good works, which God prepared in advance for us to do.

Note to Self:

____

____

____

____

____

____

Day 71

<u>Faithful with Little</u>

'Faithful with little,' is something I believe most women are accustomed to. Even if you have moved beyond that point, you have been there or maybe you watched your mama doing her thing with the little that was available, and wasn't she awesome? I didn't grow up with plenty and frankly I'm still trying to make the best of the little God has given me. However, He has promised that if we can be faithful with the little, then He will multiply the blessing into much more. I raise my hat to all you strong, smart, talented financial managers out there who have never gone to accounting school but those degree holders have nothing on you! Keep on doing your thing, God is going to bless you for your faithfulness.

Luke 16:10 (NIV) "Whoever can be trusted with very little can also be trusted with much, and whoever is dishonest with very little will also be dishonest with much.

Note to Self:

____

____

____

____

Day 72

Uncompromised Standards

We are God's children. The Bible said that He created us in His own image and likeness. This reminds me of the great love God has for us. We could have been made to look like any other creature that He had made, but he chose for us to look like Him. That is because we were meant to be family, not just another creation, but a special creation. We were created to live by God's standards and we should always be mindful of our place in this world. How do we represent our Father from day to day? Do we conform to every situation and expectation or do we stand firm on what we know is true and Godly?
My hope is that we can choose to live solely by God's standards and not by what is expected as, 'the norm'.

Romans 12:2 (NIV) Do not conform to the pattern of this world, but be transformed by the renewing of your mind. Then you will be able to test and approve what God's will is—his good, pleasing and perfect will.

Note to Self:

____

____

____

____

____

Day 73

<u>Small Group</u>

There's value in living life connected to healthy communities, and as I've said before, God did not mean for us to do life alone. We are our brother's keeper and getting connected through our churches to smaller units where everyone has the responsibility of looking out for the other is absolutely priceless. The Bible cautions us not to neglect to gather together as saints. When we do, we create cells that are bound together through the vines of righteousness and love as God intended. If you are not yet a member of a local church, I implore you to get connected with one and immediately ask about their small groups. Get involved, and allow good, Godly people to sew into you and help you find your calling and purpose.

Hebrews 10:24-25 (NIV) And let us consider how we may spur one another on toward love and good deeds, not giving up meeting together, as some are in the habit of doing, but encouraging one another—and all the more as you see the Day approaching.

Note to Self:

____

____

____

____

____

Day 74

Get into Position

Sometimes it may feel as if we are fighting against our very selves. We start every day expecting it to be different from the day before, but instead of that grand change that we desire, things either end up being exactly the same or sadly, worse! It is unbelievable that we keep on going, but we do. We believe that one day God is going to show up in a miraculous way and He will. His time and ours are so absolutely different! His ways are not like our ways and His thoughts are not like our thoughts. When the time is just right that change that you are expecting will come. Don't give up on that hope that has been pushing you forward. Get into position because you will not be able to contain what God has in store if you remain faithful and expectant.

1 Corinthian 15:57 (NIV) But thanks be to God! He gives us the victory through our Lord Jesus Christ.

Note to Self:

____

____

____

____

____

Day 75

<u>What's Your View?</u>

It is very important for us to see things through the awesome eyes of God. This however, is never easy as God's ways cannot really be fathomed by human comprehension. So then, what do we do? We read His word, pray and believe that He will reveal His view point to us in time. Always remember that God cannot be rushed! So, if you are in a hurry, you may find yourself on the wrong side of things. How we view the situations we find ourselves in will determine how we resolve the problems and move forward. Many times, what may seem like a huge blunder or setback to someone may be seen as a simple life lesson to another. Who will move forward faster? It's all about how you view the situation; do you see a lesson or a setback?

Proverbs 24:32 (NIV) I applied my heart to what I observed
and learned a lesson from what I saw.

Note to Self:

____

____

____

____

____

75

Day 76

<u>The Destructive Nature of Jealousy</u>

Here is a topic worth exploring. I am a woman and I have experienced jealousy, yea, there it is. I said it! It may not have been detrimental jealousy but jealousy none the same. We sometimes find ourselves looking at what our friends have. "How did she manage to get that nice husband or that great job or that lovely car or house?' Or whatever it might be.
We are real people living in a real world and it happens. This however, is not the heart of God and we must guard our hearts against such envious behaviour. It will only lead us into deeper, darker habits that are against God's desires. Be thankful for what you have and wait. While you wait, celebrate with others as they step into their God given blessings!

1 Corinthians 3:3 (ESV) For you are still of the flesh. For while there is jealousy and strife among you, are you not of the flesh and behaving only in a human way?

Note to Self:

____

____

____

____

____

Day 77

Growth Mindset

A growth mindset is extremely important for Godly people. When we became Christians, we were but little babies; babies in the faith. We lacked knowledge and wisdom and needed to be taught, just like a new baby trying to walk and talk. The same thing happens as we enter a post secondary education program and ultimately our careers. If we lack a growth mindset, we will find ourselves behind everyone else who desires to learn and grow. God expects His children to grow in all aspects of life, not just our Christian life but also in our social and relational lives. He wants us to be our best self. A growth mindset is extremely important to this process. Change your mindset, change your life!

Romans 12:2 (NIV) Do not conform to the pattern of this world, but be transformed by the renewing of your mind. Then you will be able to test and approve what God's will is—his good, pleasing and perfect will.

Note to Self:

____

____

____

____

____

Day 78

<u>Dealing with Distance</u>

This is a personal topic for me as I deal with the separation from my husband because of the nature of his job, on a regular basis. He spends several days working away from home which many times cause anxiety for the entire family; not just us but our children as well. These situations are never easy, but I find hope in the book of Romans as we are reminded that our present suffering will not be able to be compared to the reward that lies ahead. I have to constantly remind myself that this is but a season and seasons change. This is only a temporary situation that although unpleasant now will bring us into a season of much blessing. If you are in a similar season; distance from husband, distance from family or kids, take courage as we pray for one another and embrace this piece of the puzzle in God's perfect plan for our lives.

Romans 8:18 (NIV) I consider that our present sufferings are not worth comparing with the glory that will be revealed in us.

Note to Self:

____

____

____

____

____

Day 79

<u>Appreciating Differences</u>

It is important for us to see the differences in others and embrace them as something beautiful, rather than something to compete with or completely annihilate! I smile as I write about differences as I have had firsthand experience with how we treat others that are seen as, 'different.' I once lived in a country where we were only classified as, 'a foreigner.' You were never allowed to feel welcomed and that really hurt my heart. It shouldn't matter where someone is from, or the colour of their skin, or the texture of their hair. We are all God's and he wants us to embrace everyone with all their differences. That's His way of adding spice to our lives. Don't see others as a threat but as a blessing!

Romans 14:13 (NIV) Therefore, let us stop passing judgment on one another. Instead, make up your mind not to put any stumbling block or obstacle in the way of a brother or sister.

Note to Self:

____

____

____

____

____

Day 80

<u>Social Distancing</u>

The Covid 19 pandemic that hit, has shaken our entire world, and in the past four months has left social distancing being our new norm. A people who were made to be social beings are now being warned that being less than six feet of each other puts us at risk! This has been a devastating time, but it reminds me that I should not take the simple things in life for granted. Our church doors were closed and worship became an online affair. Thank God that He has promised that not one of His word will pass away, and so we rejoice that we are back worshipping together in His sanctuary regardless of how different that may look. We are called to be one, so let us as sisters find those who need a holy embrace, those who may be going through a rough patch, and be their strength in troubled times.

Matthew 18:20 (NIV) For where two or three gather in my name, there am I with them.

Note to Self:

____

____

____

____

____

____

Day 81

<u>Happy Hour</u>

My second son; Matthew is what I call, 'our happy hour kid.' Matthew is fifteen years old now and no longer asks as much as he use to, but growing up he would always instigate family night. This is important ladies! When our kids ask for the same thing many times, we need to make time. I must confess that we haven't made enough time to do this very important thing. Please don't make the same mistake. Spending time together as a family, playing with, and bonding with our kids is a blessing. They do not remain kids for very long. I look at my kids now and I have regrets. They are so grown and there is still so much we need to do together that we haven't done. If you have been making family time a reality, I salute you but if you need to put some things in place like myself, then today is a good day to start!

Psalm 127:3-4 (KJV) Lo, children are an heritage of the LORD: and the fruit of the womb is his reward. As arrows are in the hand of a mighty man; so are children of the youth.

Note to Self:

____

____

____

____

81

Day 82

Date Night

How's your marriage? Do you just answer right off the top or do you find yourself asking the question a second time? (Smile) Well, I can personally say, "It's not the worst but it could be better." Here's the thing ladies, we are all fired up during dating and maybe even for a few years after the wedding, but then the kids begin to show up and just when we need it the most, we stop! We stop dating. We become too busy for each other. The kids take priority, our jobs take priority and the spark vanishes without us even recognizing. Date night is very important for married couples. The kids and the jobs are very important but it shouldn't replace your love for one another. Make it a habit to plan and execute frequent date nights. Just the two of you and watch the spark re-appear. Everything will seem so much more manageable when the two of you are knitted together in love as you did when it all started.

Ephesians 5:25 (KJV) Husbands, love your wives, even as Christ also loved the church, and gave himself for it.

Note to Self:

____

____

____

____

____

Day 83

The Application Process

I've had to do many applications in my life and I am sure there will be many more. Applications seem to come with everything. Schools, jobs, loans; you name it, there's an application process attached. I don't know if you're like me but they can get under my skin. While they are very necessary and some are quite simple and straight-forward others are way too wordy and intricate and can cause you to lose a brain cell or two. If that is where you are right now, I encourage you to take heart. People experience similar perplexities and it is quite normal. Rest assured that you will get through this as you have endured so many other difficult things in your life before. Call a friend if you need to and allow someone to help you through the process. Sometimes just having someone working along with you, make it all so much more manageable.

Ecclesiastes 4:9 (KJV) Two are better than one; because they have a good reward for their labour.

Note to Self:

____

____

____

____

____

Day 84

Interview Challenge

So, I went from the application process to the interview challenge and that was quite intentional. These are two of my worst enemies. No joke, I hate them both! Ask my husband and my closest friends and they will tell you that I become a complete mess when I have an up-coming interview. I experience hot flashes and I am not even menopausal. Believe me, it's really bad. I know that I am not the only woman who experiences these anxieties. Sisters, what do you do to rid yourself of these stifling jitters? You prepare, prepare and prepare some more. Make sure you know your thing inside out. If it's a job interview, do your research, get a close friend or family member to do a mock interview with you and just be ready! Have a plan of action in the event that you begin to freak out. Like someone said, imagine them naked or even with huge smiley face emoji heads. (smile)

Psalm 34:4 (KJV) I sought the LORD, and he heard me, and delivered me from all my fears.

Note to Self:

____

____

____

____

____

Day 85
<u>Change Course</u>

Have you found yourself unhappy a little too often lately? Are you crying when no one is around, but you're not quite sure why? If that's you today, then it's time to do some well needed self assessment, and the ultimate decision may be to change course. You need to however, identify what exactly is causing you to be so completely frustrated. Sometimes we find ourselves simply drifting down a path we truly didn't intend to be on in the first place but it just seems to happen. We know that no true happiness can come from it but we continue thinking, 'I'm there already so might as well continue." It's especially hard if it's a relationship or a job. These are two huge areas that can cause some brutal upset. There has to be a solution however, and it starts with you identifying the root of the problem, then dealing with it. Get help! Allow someone who you can trust to help you through the process.

Deuteronomy 31:8 (NIV) The LORD himself goes before you and will be with you; he will never leave you nor forsake you. Do not be afraid; do not be discouraged."

Note to Self:

____

____

____

____

Day 86

Emotion Has a Voice

Emotion is said to be a natural instinctive state of mind deriving from one's circumstances, mood, or relationship with others. So, our emotions change according to the frame of mind we are in. Our actions and behaviour scream out what is going on in our emotional world. As a teacher I have firsthand experience with children as we call it, 'acting out.' But why; what is causing this behaviour? Something, whether internal or external is interfering with the child's emotions thus causing a reaction. Something has caused this behaviour and more time than not, an unfavourable behaviour. This happens with us women as well; right? Of course, it does! If our husbands forget a birthday or an anniversary the voices of our emotions will come alive. Let us be mindful as women that this happens with husbands and children as well. Listen for the voices of the emotions of those most important to us.

Proverbs 4:23 (NIV) Above all else, guard your heart,
for everything you do flows from it.

Note to Self:

____

____

____

____

Day 87

<u>The Smell of Calories</u>

I want to take this opportunity to encourage those of us that are moms to bear in mind that our kids need to feel our presence at home. I know we are super humans and we think we can do it all but find the time to indulge them. Bake with them and I say bake because it is one of our favourites but you know your kids best. You know what they like to do; go to the beach, play a game, or go for a walk on the park. Be purposeful about it and make time to do these things with them. My kids love to bake cookies and I enjoy doing that with them or sometimes just sitting back and allowing them to go at it alone is good too. (smile) This is a picture of God's heart. He is always available and ready to be all up into what we want to do, so let Him!

Ecclesiastes 8:15 (NIV) So I commend the enjoyment of life, because there is nothing better for a person under the sun than to eat and drink and be glad. Then joy will accompany them in their toil all the days of the life God has given them under the sun.

Note to Self:

____

____

____

____

____

Day 88

The Novelty of Fitness

We often hear that our bodies are the temple of the Holy Spirit. I am not sure how intentional we are about taking care of our bodies but we should be. I am not professing to be the most health conscious, but I have come to understand the need to be. Wisdom does come with age and I believe I'm beginning to gain some (smile). The novelty of fitness should never wear off. It is important that we recognize our bodies as something to be cared for. Two of the most rewarding ways to care for our bodies is through rest and exercise. More importantly ladies, to feed it with the word of God! When we are physically, emotionally and mentally fit, we are more capable of carrying out the purposes He has put in place for us to accomplish.

1 Corinthians 3:17 (NIV) If anyone destroys God's temple, God will destroy that person; for God's temple is sacred, and you together are that temple.

Note to Self:

____

____

____

____

____

Day 89

<u>Health Matters</u>

Health and fitness go hand in hand, and it's extremely important to ensure that your health is part of your priority as you embark on servicing God's temple. The fact is without good health, we have nothing! If we have poor health then we are unable to be as productive as we would like. We must therefore make every effort to remain healthy and strong. There are times when we have no control over what befalls us, but the control we do have, is to take the necessary precautions. Our yearly physicals, mammograms and pap smears for example are very important ones. Eat right, exercise and yes, rest! Please, don't forget to laugh, laugh a lot and pray a lot. All these things and more contribute to our overall health. Our health is our responsibility so take charge!

3 John 1:2 (NIV) Dear friend, I pray that you may enjoy good health and that all may go well with you, even as your soul is getting along well.

Note to Self:

____

____

____

____

____

Day 90

<u>There are no Impossibilities</u>

I have been through so many stages in my 40 plus years on this earth and there were times when all I could see were all that was impossible! I could not see anything clearly as I was looking completely through human vision! Can I tell you today that you can have 20/20 vision when you rely solely on the vision of God? It took me some time, but I've learnt that my limited vision won't do. You need a greater scope of things and He alone can offer that with 100% success rate! Nothing is impossible with God and He wants you to make Him the author and finisher of every situation you are in today. I encourage you to turn it all over to Him and watch Him turn what you thought was impossible into possibilities and accomplishments!

Jeremiah 32:17 (NIV) "Ah, Sovereign LORD, you have made the heavens and the earth by your great power and outstretched arm. Nothing is too hard for you.

Note to Self:

____

____

____

____

____

Day 91

<u>Happy to be Home</u>

I've often heard the saying, 'Home is where the heart is,' and I believe it to be quite true. I've lived in a foreign country for over eighteen years but there are times when I get that deep burning desire to go home to my homeland, Jamaica. The same thing happens when I'm out of my house for a while. I soon begin to feel the need to go home. We should be happy to be in our own homes and it is our responsibility ladies to make our homes a place our husbands and children are happy to come home to. It should be our place of refuge and solace. When things begin to fall apart, or there seem to be dangers around, our kids should be able to go home where there is safety. Safety however, depends on foundation. We must ensure that God is the foundation on which we build our homes and our lives. Only then can we have true happiness in our homes.

Matthew 7:25 (NIV) The rain came down, the streams rose, and the winds blew and beat against that house; yet it did not fall, because it had its foundation on the rock.

Note to Self:

____

____

____

____

____

Day 92

Directed Prayer

Why do we pray? The truth is, we pray because we believe that someone is listening and we hope that that person will answer us. Am I correct? I believe I am and that is why I do it as well. If I wasn't convinced of God's presence around me then maybe I wouldn't prolong that behaviour. Some of us, like me, grew up hearing and learning about God, so we know He's there. Directed prayer is very important to me. This is where I approach God's throne for something in particular! Many persons experience this kind of praying when they are struck with terminal illnesses like cancer or some other debilitating condition. Then we pray for healing specifically. However, directed prayers are not just for when you are ill. If there is something that you need to seek God about, go ahead, direct your prayer towards that and believe!

1 John 5:14-15 (NIV) This is the confidence we have in approaching God: that if we ask anything according to his will, he hears us. And if we know that he hears us—whatever we ask—we know that we have what we asked of him.

Note to Self:

____

____

____

____

Day 93

It's Not a Competition

I grab my topics from different places and yesterday I was having some down time watching a movie about two sisters who had gone on a vacation together and found themselves in a very dangerous place at the bottom of the ocean with killer sharks swimming around them. One sister got the opportunity to confess that she had always been jealous of her sister's ability to venture out, take risks and live vicariously. She was the opposite and getting married and settling down was the one thing she had above her sister. Her husband had just left her and she was devastated. Here they were now in the midst of danger due to jealousy. What grabbed me was the sister's response. She looked her in the eye and said, 'It was never a competition!' For some it isn't but for others it is. Let us be mindful of these feelings that can creep in and cause destruction. Let us identify them and deal with them before they actually become destructive.

Galatians 6:4 (NIV) Each one should test their own actions. Then they can take pride in themselves alone, without comparing themselves to someone else,

Note to Self:

____

____

____

____

Day 94

<u>Be Set Free</u>

It has been a great honour to encourage your minds and spirits, and today I implore you to be free! Free from sin, from blame, from setbacks, from disappointments, from unaccomplished dreams and all that would hinder your progress. I declare healing over your mind and spirit and I call upon the forces of heaven to break every chain of bondage from your life. I pray for generational curses to be broken and for the spirit of the Holy Ghost to engulf and take over, take over where division was, where hurt and pain segregated for years, where feelings of inadequacy lingered, and where the lie of inferiority was. God, in the mighty name of Jesus Christ of Nazareth I pray for a complete 360 degree turn of events in the lives of my sisters. Loose, be loose Holy Spirit in the mighty name of Jesus.

Romans 6:22 (NIV) But now that you have been set free from sin and have become slaves of God, the benefit you reap leads to holiness, and the result is eternal life.

Note to Self:

____

____

____

____

____

Day 95

<u>Simply Ask</u>

We receive not because we ask not! It is important for us to understand the importance of asking! The Bible says that we should ask of God what we want. It states that He already knows what we have need of, yet He desires us to ask! Don't we as mothers do the same to our children? I know I do. It's a good lesson that is being taught. There are several lessons to be learnt from this exercise. The first is to be humble enough to ask, and the second is to ask with the right attitude if they are expecting to receive. The same principle applies with our Father in Heaven. Here are a few questions I now ask myself before approaching my Father in heaven. What am I requesting? Why do I want it and how will it be used to bless the lives of others? See, asking is one thing; our motives must be in line with His will as well. Ask in confidence believing that God will answer if it is in His will. I would like to believe that it is our desire to live in His will.

Mark 11:24 (NIV) Therefore, I tell you, whatever you ask for in prayer, believe that you have received it, and it will be yours.

Note to Self:

____

____

____

____

____

Day 96

<u>It is not your Aptitude but you Attitude that Determines your Altitude</u>

As I write on this profound topic, I think of the wise lady that instilled it within me during my high school years; Mrs. Joan Wint! This astute lady was the principal of my school; Denbigh High, in May Pen Clarendon, Jamaica. Without even knowing it, she has been a driving force behind my success. She repeated that fact as often as I can remember during our general devotional exercises until it was etched in the cells of my brain. There was no erasing it and I am forever grateful! I now live by that fact. In fact, it is my motto and my success statement! What is your attitude today? Is it keeping you from your success? If it is then, go ahead borrow my motto and make that needed change!

Philippians 4:8 (KJV) Finally, brethren, whatsoever things are true, whatsoever things are honest, whatsoever things are just, whatsoever things are pure, whatsoever things are lovely, whatsoever things are of good report; if there be any virtue, and if there be any praise, think on these things.

Note to Self:

____

____

____

____

Day 97

<u>Grace on Top of Grace</u>

I sometimes ask myself, how did I get here, what did I do to deserve this or who am I that the Sovereign God would give thought of me? My heart begins to swell really big when I begin to truly assess who I am, how unworthy I have been and how completely blessed I am none the less. My heart is not big enough or strong enough to embrace the love of God! There is no understanding how someone so sinful and wretched could be so completely loved and cherished by a perfect God. With huge tear drops in my eyes and a throbbing deep in my chest I acknowledge that it has nothing at all to do with me or with you. It is simply grace on top of grace! If you are feeling the same today, go ahead and give Him all the praise He so truly deserves!

Ephesians 2:4-5 (NIV) But because of his great love for us, God, who is rich in mercy, made us alive with Christ even when we were dead in transgressions—it is by grace you have been saved.

Note to Self:

____

____

____

____

____

____

Day 98

<u>Feel the Intensity</u>

I haven't always been close to God! I grew up in church and I've always acknowledged that there is a God to be feared, but still I sinned and did what I knew I shouldn't do. I received water baptism at age sixteen but didn't completely live, 'the life.' I try to 'cut the teenagers some slack,' as I know how it feels to just want to fit in. We can still pray for them and lead them the best way we can to a God who is the, 'Koolest!' It took me many years to feel that intensity of love that God offers. I couldn't see it, so I couldn't feel it and now that I have, I feel so disappointed that I wasted all those years going my own way and doing my own thing. Having a close, intimate relationship with God is beyond anything you could ever experience!

Psalm 25:4-5 (NIV) Show me your ways, LORD, teach me your paths. Guide me in your truth and teach me, for you are God my Savior, and my hope is in you all day long.

Note to Self:

____

____

____

____

____

Day 99

<u>Sold</u>

How are you feeling today? Take a deep breath, you are almost there! I am so happy that you decided to go all the way; the whole 100 days. My hope is that you took it one day at a time, reading and making short notes to yourself. If you did, I'm praying that something has changed and that you are, 'sold,' on what us, as ladies, need to be doing. There is no quick fix to anything in life, but I believe if you open up and allow God to do a mighty work on the inside then nothing in your present or future life will ever be the same again. I feel so privileged to have gone on this journey with you and now we are forever bonded together as sisters in Christ. You will forever be in my heart and my prayers as I approach the throne of God daily you will be in my focus point. Release and be free!

John 3:16 (KJV) For God so loved the world, that he gave his only begotten Son, that whosoever believeth in him should not perish, but have everlasting life.

Note to Self:

____

____

____

____

____

Day 100

All of This for Your Glory!

This book came into existence merely out of God prompting me in this direction. I didn't plan it for years and I didn't spend years writing it. He simply instructed me to write and I started and here we are. It is my great hope that these entries would have blessed you in one form or the other to believe that you are loved by God and that He has put people in place here on earth to share in your exciting journey. He didn't promise a perfect life. He promised a protected life. So, trust Him today and allow Him to create or re-create what is needed for you to acknowledge His will and step into your purpose, and may all the glory go to Him in Calvary!

1 Corinthians 10:31-33 (NIV) So, whether you eat or drink or whatever you do, do it all for the glory of God. Do not cause anyone to stumble, whether Jews, Greeks or the church of God, even as I try to please everyone in every way. For I am not seeking my own good but the good of many, so that they may be saved.

Note to Self:

____

____

____

____

____

O'Nesseia has been an elementary school educator for over twenty years, and has great passion for working with children. She has never really thought about seriously writing a book. She has toyed with the idea of maybe someday writing an autobiography or children's books but never a devotional or even more personal, a motivational book. However, God has never ceased to amaze her and she can tell He's not about to stop now!

This is by far the most amazing and 'wild thing,' He has called her to do. She was completely blown away, asking God, "Are you sure, me?" But she didn't want to seem disobedient and she surely didn't want to lose her blessing being 'a doubtful Thomas.' There were days when she was so afraid, so tentative, asking God if this was really him, and if she should really be doing this. She would feel so empowered one day and the next totally hesitant and fearful.

The fact of the matter is, she knew nothing about writing a book! Negative thoughts flooded her mind such as, it may never get published, or no one would like or even want to read it. She wondered if it would be beneficial to anyone and if it was truly worth the effort. In spite of her doubts, the more she thought about it, the more she was reminded that it wasn't about her. It was God's work, not hers. She was only being used as His hands, His voice. So, she knew that what He started, He would bring to completion and by extension success! If this book helps one woman to overcome her fears, re-discover or discover her worth then it would have been the greatest success and she would be proud to have been used by God in this way.

O'Nesseia and her husband Oral have three children; two sons; O'Tave Kevin and O'Ryan Matthew and their precious gem, a daughter; O'Riyah Hanna-Maria.